NATIONAL GEOGRAPHIC

Ladders

GRAND CANYON National Park

GENRE Social Studies Article **Read to find out** how Grand Canyon National Park came to exist.

Welcome to the GRAND

by Amy Weber

You are standing at the edge of one of the natural wonders of the world, the Grand Canyon, gazing at colorful layers of rock. Did you know that you are looking at two billion years of Earth's history? Each rock layer in this massive **canyon** represents a different time in the life of our planet.

The canyon was created by water and time. Geologists—scientists who study the history of Earth—believe the Colorado River began carving the canyon about six million years ago. The river carried huge amounts of sand and gravel that helped it cut deeply into the land.

Even before the river began its work, wind and water carried **minerals**, sand, mud, and even the remains of tiny ocean creatures to this area and deposited them in layers. Over millions of years, these layers hardened into rock. Today they are a valuable record of our planet's history. Grand Canyon National Park was created to preserve and protect this record.

From your perch on the rim, it is clear that the Grand Canyon is one of the largest canyons on Earth. The Colorado River flows about a mile below you on the canyon's floor. The canyon winds its way for 277 miles through the high Arizona Desert. It would take you five hours to drive this distance in a car if the road were flat and straight. This really is a grand canyon!

CANYON

Notice the different-colored layers of rocks. Each one represents a different time in Earth's history. See the Colorado River in the middle of the photograph? The oldest, deepest layer of rock in the canyon is found along the river. This layer is about two billion years old.

This close-up shows colorful rock layers in the Grand Canyon. Some were made of sand and mud, and some were made of ancient sea creatures. Over hundreds of millions of years, this loose material was pressed together into hard rock layers. Millions of years later, the Colorado River began carving its way through this area, wearing away the rock to form the canyon. The deeper it cut into the rock, the more layers were revealed.

History of the Park

The human history of this natural wonder began long before Spanish explorers first saw the Grand Canyon in the mid-1500s. Native American groups, such as the Havasupai (hah-vuh-SOO-py), have made the canyon their home for at least 800 years. Even today, some Native American groups live within the canyon, outside the boundaries of the national park.

The chance to find gold, silver, and other mineral riches drew many **prospectors** to the canyon area in the 1800s, but mining there was harsh and difficult. One prospector, John Hance, had another idea. He began leading tours into the canyon. Soon his canyon tours attracted many curious sightseers. Other prospectors and fortune seekers realized they could make more money leading tours and feeding visitors than they ever could by mining.

After President Theodore Roosevelt visited the canyon in 1903, he worked to make it a national preserve. That's a place where the animals are protected from hunters. The Grand Canyon became a national park in 1919. This helped protect the canyon's land and wildlife from people who wanted to mine it, hunt within it, or build private homes and hotels at its edge.

^ **The Havasupai people have lived for hundreds of years near Havasu Falls in a side canyon of the Grand Canyon. They still live there. They have always worked to preserve the region's habitats and wildlife, a goal the United States adopted by establishing the national park in 1919.**

1540

Led by a Native American guide, Spanish explorers are the first Europeans to see the canyon. They find no gold or silver in the area.

1776

Spanish priest Francisco Garcés travels to the Grand Canyon and meets the Havasupai. The Havasupai also meet the canyon's first tourists.

1869

Major John Wesley Powell leads an expedition down the Colorado River. He names the Grand Canyon as he and his crew travel through it.

1901

The first train service in the area brings tourists from Williams, Arizona, to the South Rim of the Grand Canyon.

1919

The U.S. Congress establishes Grand Canyon National Park to preserve the canyon's land and wildlife.

1996

Six California condors are released near the canyon. These birds were once nearly extinct, but today they are protected here in the park.

2011

More than 4 million visitors flock to see the views and explore the rugged beauty of Grand Canyon.

A Natural Wonder

There aren't many hikes that take you through both chilly, shady forests and searing desert heat. That's what it's like to hike from the North Rim of the Grand Canyon, with its cool evergreen forests, to the hot desert scrublands near the bottom of the canyon. Since the canyon is so deep and so wide, there are amazingly different habitats and natural environments between the rim of the **gorge**, or steep-sided canyon, and the canyon's floor, on the banks of the Colorado River.

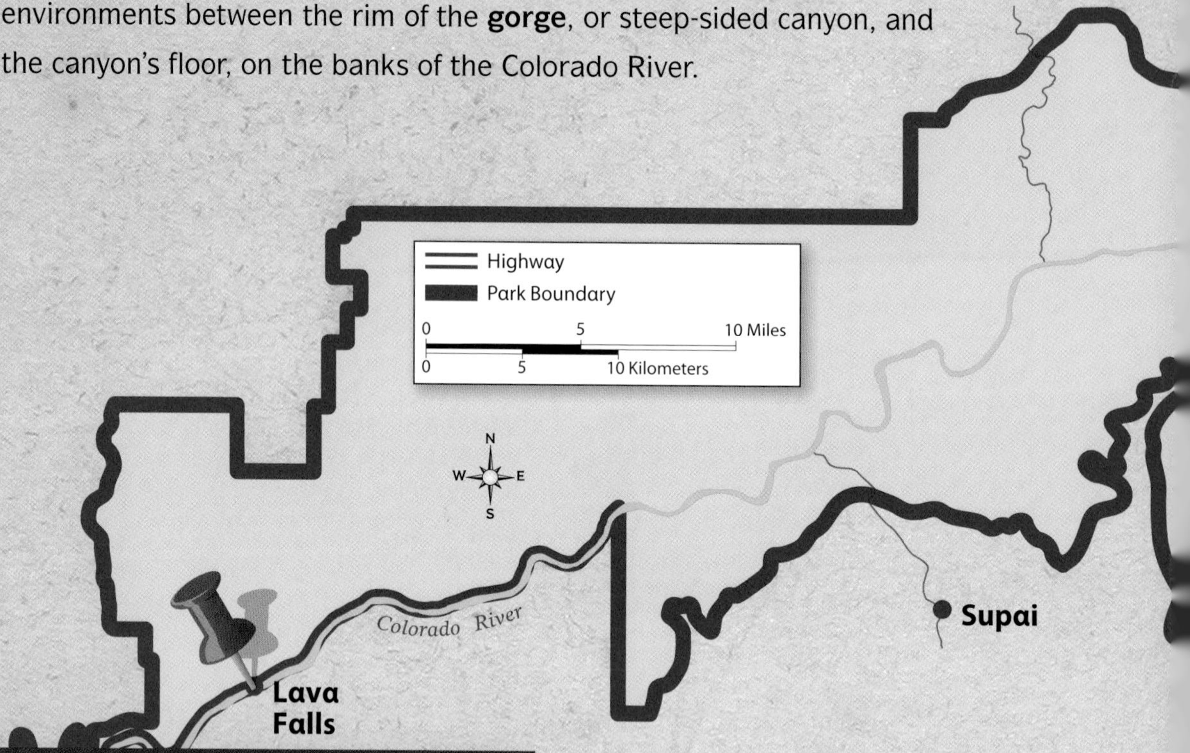

LAVA FALLS

Rafters both love and fear Lava Falls. It's the most dangerous rapids in all of the Grand Canyon. Strap down your gear and hold on to your paddle!

Today's plants and animals aren't the only canyon features that change the deeper you go. The oldest fossils here date back more than a billion years. Most of these fossils are creatures that lived in ancient seas that once covered this land. The deeper you hike, the farther back in time you're traveling. But don't expect to find dinosaur bones at the Grand Canyon. The canyon's youngest rocks are 270 million years old. They were formed long before any dinosaur roamed on Earth.

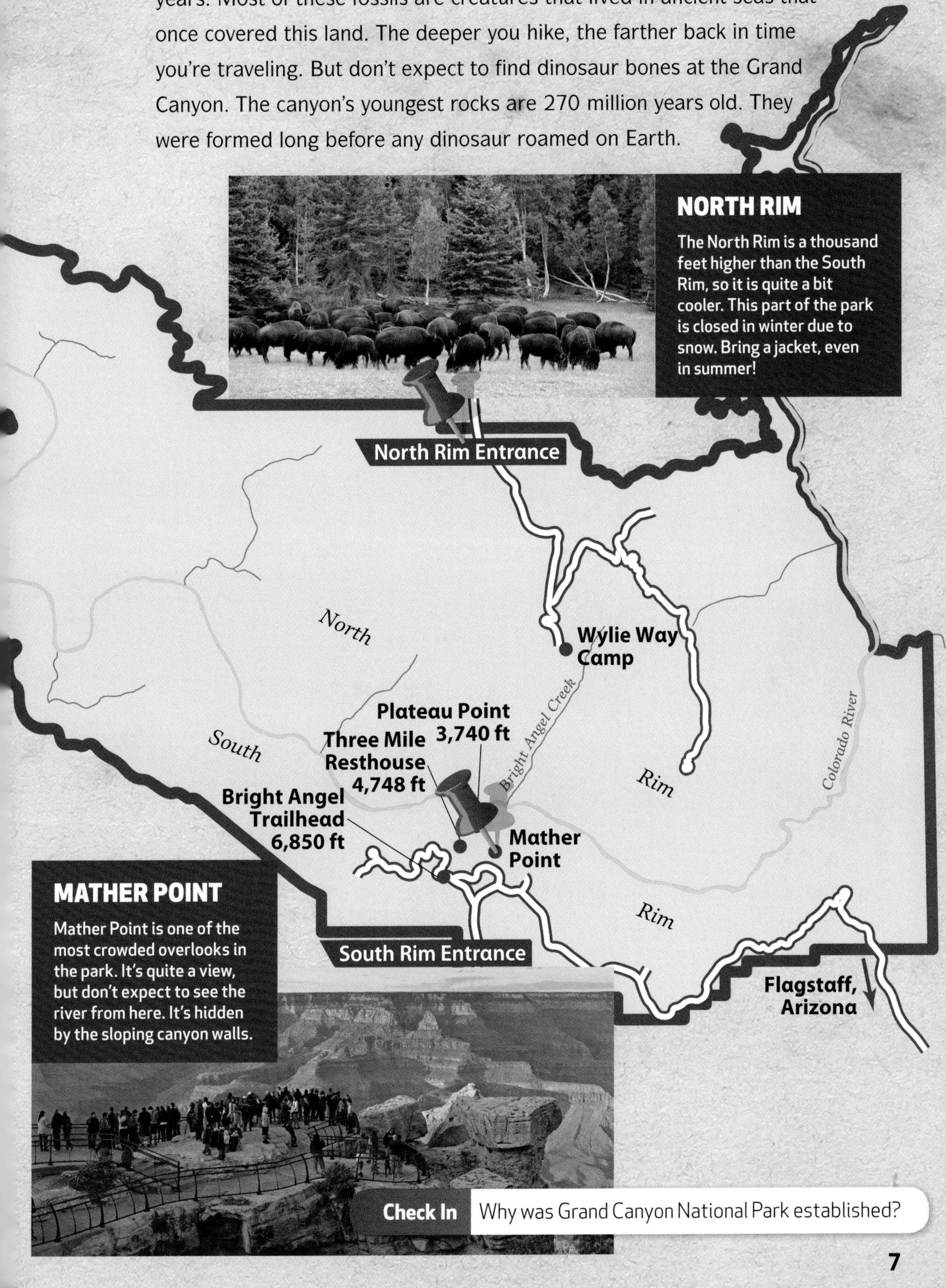

NORTH RIM

The North Rim is a thousand feet higher than the South Rim, so it is quite a bit cooler. This part of the park is closed in winter due to snow. Bring a jacket, even in summer!

MATHER POINT

Mather Point is one of the most crowded overlooks in the park. It's quite a view, but don't expect to see the river from here. It's hidden by the sloping canyon walls.

Check In Why was Grand Canyon National Park established?

GENRE Geography Tour

Read to find out about he features unique to the Grand Canyon.

Hike Down the Canyo

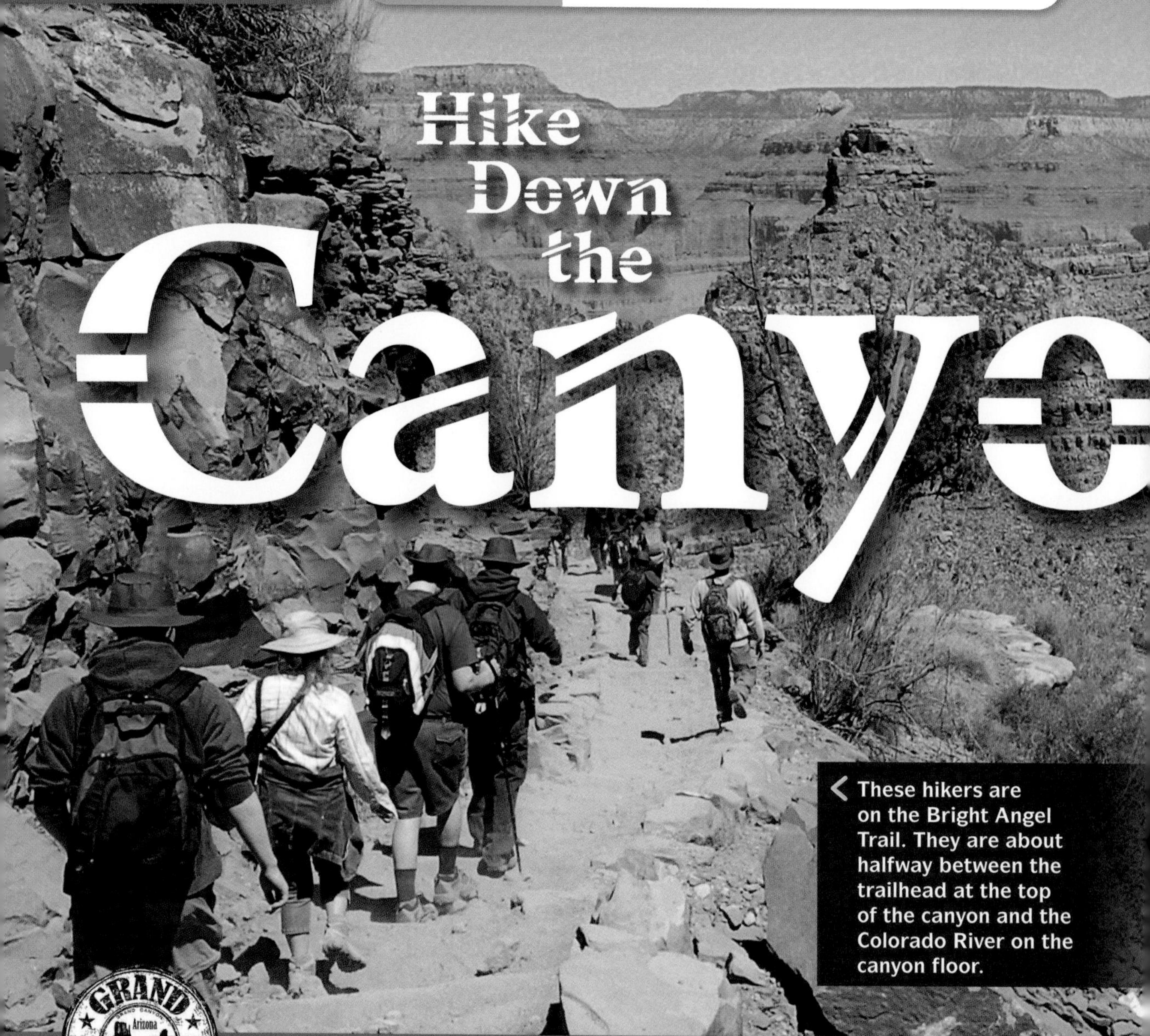

These hikers are on the Bright Angel Trail. They are about halfway between the trailhead at the top of the canyon and the Colorado River on the canyon floor.

Bright Angel Trailhead | Elevation: 6,850 feet

You can't see the Colorado River from where you stand up high at the Bright Angel Trailhead, but you know it's there, about a mile below you. The river is our goal for today. Do you have enough food and water? How about a sun hat and sturdy shoes? Breathe in the scent of those ponderosa pines because we're about to leave the shady forests of the South Rim behind and step into a harsh, breathtaking desert.

Gaze out over the canyon as we start hiking downward below the rim. Look at the colorful rock layers, or **strata**, that paint the canyon red, purple, and gold. These horizontal strata are **sedimentary rocks**, made up of sediment, or small particles of sand, mud, and the remains of tiny creatures. This sediment was deposited by wind, water, and ice and then squeezed into rock over millions of years.

n

by Becky Manfredini

The change in elevation is nearly a mile between the South Rim at the top of the canyon and the Colorado River at the bottom. Elevation is height above sea level. This chart shows the elevation at each stop on the hike.

On the first part of our hike, the canyon walls are so steep that the trail zigzags down a long series of switchbacks, or sharp turns, that take us down into the gorge. Let's pause a bit to take a good look at one of the first landmarks on the trail. It's a wall filled with pictographs, which are rock paintings of symbols, people, and animals made hundreds of years ago by the Native Americans who once lived here.

The color of the canyon wall changes as we hike deeper. The creamy gray rock high at the rim of the canyon is the Kaibab Formation, the canyon's top layer. It formed about 270 million years ago. That's a long time ago—long before the first dinosaur lived—but it's the youngest rock layer in the canyon! As we hike through the strata, imagine what the view was like when each layer was forming.

South Rim
Coconino Sandstone
Hermit Shale

Three Mile Resthouse | Elevation: 4,748 feet

Below the Kaibab Formation is a thick, beige cliff called the Coconino Sandstone. This layer was originally sand dunes on the shore of an ancient sea. Because it is so light in color, some folks call this the "bathtub ring" of the Grand Canyon. See if you can spy some animal tracks in the rocks by the trail. They weren't made today, or even yesterday. They are fossils. They were probably made by creatures similar to today's desert scorpions.

As the switchbacks take us farther down into the canyon, we pass through the Hermit Shale, formed from silt and mud laid down in ancient streams. We also hike our way down through strata that look like many tiny stair steps. The strata represent a time of rapidly changing sea levels. Some layers of strata were sand dunes long ago, while others were beaches and even ocean floors. Fossil hunters have found the remains of many burrowing creatures here.

Finally, we have hiked far enough down to reach the top of the Redwall Limestone, a 500-foot-thick layer of rock formed mostly from prehistoric ocean life. We've hiked three miles down into the canyon already. It's good that we can take a break at Three Mile Resthouse. Let's fill our water bottles, sit in the shade for a moment, and gaze up at the South Rim, now far above us. Get ready, though, because we're about to hike down those steep Redwall cliffs.

Plateau Point | Elevation: 3,740 feet

We continue our hike down the canyon. Near the foot of the Redwall Limestone cliffs, we reach an oasis, an area with trees, a spring, and fresh water. It's called Indian Garden because Native Americans used to farm here long ago. It's a good place to rest, picnic, or camp overnight. Reaching Indian Garden means we're halfway down the Bright Angel Trail, but we're going to take a short detour out to Plateau Point.

It's about a mile and a half out to Plateau Point. Just look at the view! It looks like there's a whole mountain range inside the canyon. These peaks, towers, and **buttes** (BYOOTZ)—steep hills with flat tops—became separated from the canyon walls as streams and rivers cut through different parts of the land. People today have given them names such as Battleship Butte. Can you see why?

We're walking on top of yet another layer of rock—the Bright Angel Shale. This greenish rock was formed in a shallow sea filled with life around 515 million years ago. We haven't seen the river yet, and this layer is the reason. It hides the river from us until we stand at Plateau Point. Look down. The river is still very far below us, but you can see how powerful it is. After all, it carved this entire canyon.

Let's retrace our steps to Indian Garden and stop for a picnic lunch of our own. Then fill your water bottle again and prepare yourself because we're about to hike down into the inner gorge. There's no source of water or shade between here and the river, and the trail will be hot, winding, and steep. Just remember, good food and a comfortable bed are waiting at the end of the trail.

Colorado River | Elevation: 1,300 feet

We've finally reached the bottom of the canyon! At the foot of the Bright Angel Trail, we come face-to-face with the architect of the Grand Canyon—the Colorado River. Much of the rock here is nearly two billion years old. That's about half as old as Earth itself! Let's head to the footbridge and cross the river. There's a beach where rafters are pulling their boats up for the night. We're all headed to the same place.

The Phantom Ranch is where hikers, mule riders, and river rafters meet to rest before they continue their journeys. Here, we can eat a hearty meal in the dining hall and get a good night's sleep in a cabin or a bunkhouse. The canyon walls rise up nearly a mile all around us, so after the sun sets, be sure to look up into the sky. You'll see thousands of stars from down here.

We'll have to rise early tomorrow to start our return hike. Phantom Ranch is about 4,600 feet below the South Rim. You came all that way today! But tomorrow we must hike back up the Bright Angel Trail, and it will take us twice as long as it did to hike down. For now, though, grab a well-earned rest and dream of your canyon adventure.

Today we hiked through a true natural wonder—a canyon that has been shaped by the forces of nature: wind, water, and ice. Thanks to the efforts of the people who established and maintain this national park, the Grand Canyon will be protected and preserved forever for other hikers to enjoy. How lucky we are!

Check In What canyon feature do you find most interesting? Why?

GENRE Historical Fiction

Read to find out how a burro became a canyon legend.

The Story of BRIGHTY the BURRO

by Becky Manfredini *Illustrated by Max Kostenko*

There once lived a free-spirited burro that romped alongside waterways and roamed the steep trails of the Grand Canyon. He was named "Bright Angel" after the rushing Bright Angel Creek in the depths of the canyon. But he was nicknamed "Brighty" by the local people and visitors along the North Rim. Over the years, this shaggy gray burro captured the hearts of children, tourists, artists, rangers—and even the President of the United States.

In 1892, two prospectors hoped to strike it rich by mining a remote cave inside the Grand Canyon. A little gray burro traveled beside them, carrying a heavy pack of supplies. The trio made their way from Flagstaff, Arizona, to the canyon's South Rim. Under the hot sun, they plodded along a small footpath until they reached the rushing Colorado River.

Exhausted, the men set up camp; they made flapjacks and let the little burro eat his fill. Well-fed and drowsy, the burro fell asleep under the stars.

When he awoke very early in the morning, the burro left his sleeping companions to get a drink in the cold, refreshing river. All day long he played by the river. By sunset, the burro's belly was growling fiercely from hunger, so he trotted back to camp. When he got there, he let out a loud *Yeee-aww,* because he saw no campfire, no food, and no prospectors. They had disappeared.

It was clear that the men wouldn't be back, but the little burro was surprisingly delighted. No more heavy packs to carry! And who needed flapjacks? He could always munch on grass.

As days passed, the burro enjoyed his new freedom. On one particularly hot day, he trotted along the river and noticed a shallow section. Curiously and cautiously, he waded into the water and then swam to the other side.

Thrilled to have someplace new to investigate, the burro spent his days exploring the canyon's north side, splashing in Bright Angel Creek, and playing with small canyon critters. One day as he wandered into the upper region of the canyon, he found some other burros. "Maybe they can be my friends," Brighty thought; but they were much bigger and wilder than shaggy gray Brighty, so he decided to keep to himself.

After a while, Brighty did make friends in the canyon. At the North Rim, he often visited the Wylie Way Camp where many tourists spent the summer in tent-cabins. There, he met the McKee family, the caretakers at the camp, and they were kind to the little burro.

But not everyone Brighty met was so kind. One day as he stood dreaming of his next meal, Brighty spotted an explorer hiking along the trail. The little burro grew cheerful, eager to see if this new friend might feed him something delicious. But things didn't go as Brighty had hoped. Instead, the explorer captured him and strapped his gear onto the burro's back. It was a heavy load!

After a week of hard work, Brighty grew tired of the explorer and his gear. Without warning, he bucked his hind legs high in the air and threw off the heavy packs. Then he scrambled up a ridge to play a game of hide-and-seek with the frustrated explorer. The furious man chased after Brighty for hours. When he finally caught the little burro, he tied a bell around his neck so he could hear Brighty's every movement. But Brighty outsmarted the explorer yet again. He practiced stepping smoothly and lightly, keeping the bell perfectly still. Quiet as a mouse, Brighty slipped away one night, free once again.

For months, Brighty roamed the canyon, enjoying his freedom and the beautiful land around him. Then one day, he gazed up and noticed that the snow on top of the North Rim had melted in the hot sun. Like a bird, Brighty knew it was time to migrate there, where he could spend the warm weather months at Bright Angel Point.

Brighty trekked slowly back up the hot, dry canyon, stopping often to rest in cool caves and soak his sore hooves in splashing streams. As Brighty neared the North Rim, he remembered his friends, the McKees, and their lovely campground, and trotted eagerly in their direction. Before long, he spotted the McKees doing chores around the camp. He sniffed the air, smelled hot flapjacks with syrup, and let out a hearty *Yee-aw* to say hello.

After a few days of rest and flapjack eating, the little burro began helping Bobby McKee with one of his campground tasks, hauling water up from a spring below the canyon's rim. Brighty would haul heavy bags of water up to the campground without complaining, several times a day! After hours of hard labor, Brighty's thoughts would return to the heaping plate of wild berry flapjacks that would be waiting for him at the campground. He was happy working hard for kind people.

When he wasn't working or eating, Brighty romped and rolled in the nearby meadow and gave rides to children visiting the camp. One day, some bigger boys decided that they wanted Brighty to trot faster, and Brighty's patience wore thin. He kicked up his heels, lowered his head between his forelegs, and threw them off. The stubborn and strong little burro always let people know who was boss!

On one special occasion, President Teddy Roosevelt visited the North Rim to go exploring with Uncle Jim Owens, a game warden for the forest service. At night, the friends sat around the campfire while the president shared plans for creating a park, right there at the Grand Canyon.

Soon, workers arrived to make improvements in the canyon. One day, Brighty heard some unusual sounds coming from the bottom by the river. Whack! Whack! Whack! Curious, he trotted toward the hammering sound and couldn't believe his eyes. Men were busily building a bridge over the river to connect the North and South Rims. Immediately, workers enlisted Brighty and his strong back to help construct the bridge.

At last, the bridge was finished and ready for hikers and mule trains. On the day of the dedication ceremony, President Roosevelt bestowed Brighty with a special honor. Since he was the oldest and most distinguished inhabitant of the Grand Canyon, he would be the first to walk over the bridge.

From that day forward, the government made it official: Brighty would be forever free. The little burro could roam wherever he wanted without anyone capturing him again. No non-wild animal had ever been allowed to graze on national park lands—except for Brighty of the Grand Canyon.

Brighty lived in the massive canyon for almost 30 years. Although he died many years ago, the little burro's legend lives on. If you visit the North Rim, go to the sunroom at Grand Canyon Lodge. There you will see sculptor Peter Jepson's life-size bronze statue of Brighty. They say that if you rub the statue's nose, you will have good luck!

Check In Why is Brighty's story important to Grand Canyon National Park?

GENRE Social Studies Article

Read to find out about Grand Canyon adventures.

Many people visit the Grand Canyon. They stand at the edge and marvel at this natural wonder. They hike along the rim, checking out the colorful layers of rock and the towering buttes that rise in the middle of the canyon. They stay in the lodges or in trailers in comfortable campgrounds. But some people look for more rugged adventures within the canyon itself. Would you like to have one of those adventures? Let's go!

Grand Canyon ADVENTU

by Amy Weber

When you hear the term **backcountry camping**, think of it as camping far away from people and civilization—really roughing it. Backcountry campers depend entirely upon what they can fit in their backpacks. When they're done camping, they leave nothing behind, so their campsites stay exactly as they found them—natural and clean. This isn't for everyone, but seeing the canyon and its plants and wildlife up close makes it worth the effort. And sleeping under the stars in the Grand Canyon is a treat. There are more stars than you can imagine.

RES

300,418 campers

More than 300,000 campers spent the night in the Grand Canyon backcountry in 2012. That sounds like a lot, but not when you find out that almost 4.5 million people visited the park in that same year.

10 dollars

A backcountry camping permit costs $10, plus another $5 for each person camping below the rim of the canyon. That's a bargain when you consider that a trailer campsite with hookups for water and electricity costs at least $35 per night.

75 miles

If you're itching for a backcountry experience but you just can't get to the canyon, go online. Thanks to cameras that were attached to hiker's heads, you can now watch 75 miles of below-the-rim hiking on the Internet.

class 10

That's the hardest, most dangerous rapids whitewater rafters ever have to face. Lava Falls, the most challenging rapids in the canyon, are class 10. That's some rough water!

---

30 feet

That's how much the Colorado River drops at Hance Rapid, the steepest single drop of any rapids in the Grand Canyon.

---

277 river miles

The Grand Canyon is measured at 277 river miles, the distance the winding Colorado River travels through the gorge. Stretched out straight, that length of river would reach across the state of Indiana from north to south.

Thrill Ride!

Are you looking for an extreme thrill? How about riding down the 277 miles of untamed river that runs through the canyon? The 200 or so **rapids**, or stretches of fast-moving water, can take your breath away! **Whitewater rafting** is a sport that uses an inflatable raft, or small boat, to float down a river and over rapids. Shooting whitewater can feel like a wet roller-coaster ride. Water splashes all around you, even inside the raft. And when the river is calm, you can see wildlife, hidden waterfalls, and side canyons that are not visible from the canyon's rim.

200 pounds

That's the weight limit if you want to ride a mule from the rim to the river. If the hour-long trip is more your speed, you can weigh up to 220 pounds. An average mule can carry up to 230 pounds. They are strong and tough animals!

4'7" in height

You have to be 55 inches tall to take a mule ride at Grand Canyon, no matter how much riding experience you have. That's 4'7" tall. And you have to be 10 years old to ride to the river. If you're older than 7 but not quite 10, the hour-long mule ride is for you.

5.5 hours

That's about how long it takes a mule train to travel from the trailhead on the canyon's rim to the river at the bottom of the canyon. The return trip takes more like 6.5 hours. That's why mule trains stop overnight at the Phantom Ranch.

Ridin' It!

Not interested in riding the rapids or hiking? Try hitching a ride with a mule train. A mule is a cross between a horse and a donkey. It is as strong as a horse and as sure-footed as a donkey—perfect to carry riders through the steep, rocky canyon. For more than 100 years, mule trains, or groups of mules led by a guide, have carried visitors into the canyon. In fact, President Theodore Roosevelt took the trip in 1906. Mule trains consist of many mules that carry people and packs up and down these trails. Since the canyon is too steep and dangerous to build a highway, these furry animals may be the best way to go. Are you ready? Giddy-up!

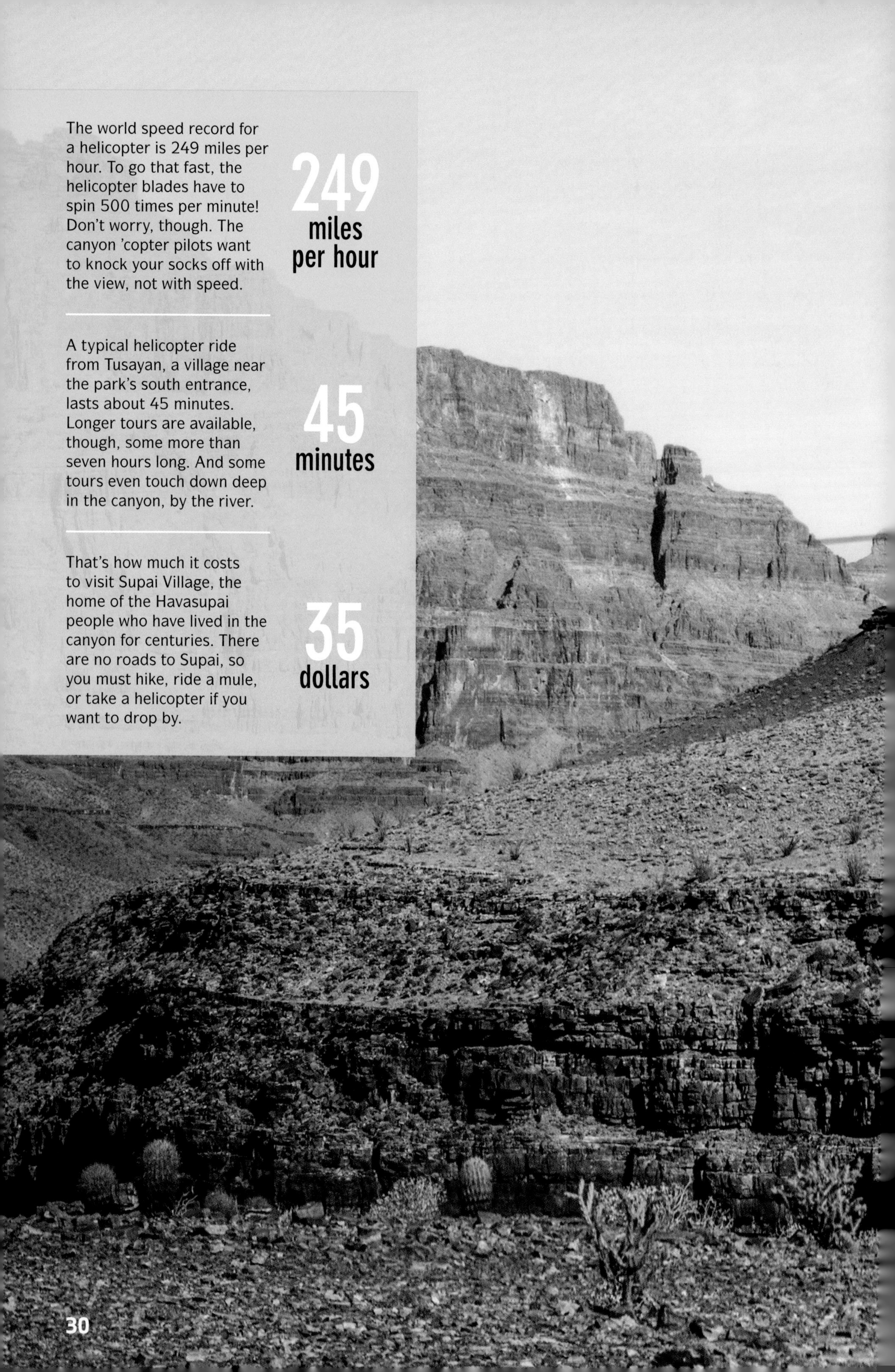

The world speed record for a helicopter is 249 miles per hour. To go that fast, the helicopter blades have to spin 500 times per minute! Don't worry, though. The canyon 'copter pilots want to knock your socks off with the view, not with speed.

249
miles per hour

A typical helicopter ride from Tusayan, a village near the park's south entrance, lasts about 45 minutes. Longer tours are available, though, some more than seven hours long. And some tours even touch down deep in the canyon, by the river.

45
minutes

That's how much it costs to visit Supai Village, the home of the Havasupai people who have lived in the canyon for centuries. There are no roads to Supai, so you must hike, ride a mule, or take a helicopter if you want to drop by.

35
dollars

Soaring!

What do eagles and falcons see as they swoop down through the crisp canyon air? You'll soon find out when you fly high above the Grand Canyon in a helicopter, looking down on the hikers, rafters, and mule trains. Helicopters can shoot up straight into the sky and hover over the canyon. They can fly at speeds of 200 miles per hour, but they slow down when they enter the canyon. Views that can take hours to see on foot take only about 20 to 60 minutes to get to by helicopter.

Check In Which adventure would you most like to have in the Grand Canyon? Why?

Discuss

1. What connections can you make among the four selections in this book? How do you think they are related?
2. How is the North Rim different from the canyon floor? Describe how the environment changes as you hike through the canyon.
3. Compare the historical fiction story of Brighty with what you've learned about the geography and history of the Grand Canyon. What parts of the story tell facts about the Grand Canyon? What parts do you think are made up? Explain your answers.
4. What are the most exciting things about touring, hiking, or camping in the Grand Canyon? What precautions must you take?
5. What do you still wonder about the Grand Canyon and about Grand Canyon National Park?